THE ZIGZAG WALK

BY JOHN LOGAN

Poetry:

Cycle for Mother Cabrini (1955)
Ghosts of the Heart (1960)
Spring of the Thief (1963)
The Zigzag Walk (1969)

For Children:
Tom Savage (1962)

E. P. DUTTON
& CO., INC.
NEW YORK
1969

THE
ZIG
ZAG
WALK

Poems:
1963-1968

JOHN
LOGAN

To the editors of the following publications in which these poems first appeared, the author makes grateful acknowledgment:

CHELSEA: "Lines on Locks"
CHICAGO REVIEW: "Two Preludes for La Push"
CHOICE: "Three Moves," "Love Poem," "Letter to a Young Father in Exile"
THE FAIR: "The Owl"
GALLERY SERIES ONE: "Twilight Land"
Heartland: Poets of the Midwest, edited by Lucien Stryk, "Elegy for the Rev. Mr. James B. Hodgson," © 1967 Northern Illinois University Press.
THE HUDSON REVIEW: "The Pass," "Sebastian in the Dream"
JEOPARDY: "Thirteen Preludes for Pioneer Square"
JOURNAL OF CREATIVE BEHAVIOR: "San Francisco Poem"
KAYAK: "On the House of a Friend"
THE MINNESOTA REVIEW: "The Zoo," "David and Isabel" (Homage to Herman Melville)
THE NATION: "Lines for a Young Man Who Talked," "Prison Poem," "White Pass Ski Patrol," "The Search"
NEW MEXICO QUARTERLY: "Grandmother Dead in the Aeroplane"
NEW UNIVERSITY THOUGHT: "They've Blocked Every Window"
THE NEW YORKER: "The Rescue," © 1966, The New Yorker Magazine, Inc.
THE NORTH AMERICAN REVIEW: "Suzanne," "The Weeping"
THE NORTHWEST REVIEW: "Three Poems on Morris Graves' Paintings"
POETRY: "On the Death of Keats," "Carmel: Point Lobos," "Big Sur: Partington Cove"
QUARTERLY REVIEW OF LITERATURE: "Lines for Michael in the Picture"
THE SEWANEE REVIEW: "Poem, Slow to Come, on the Death of Cummings," © 1967, The University of the South
THE SULLIVAN SLOUGH REVIEW: "Helian"

For my father, my brother, my six sons
and for Michael.

CONTENTS

9

1

THE ZOO

1

Like a child the wise porpoise
at the Brookfield Zoo plays
in the continuous, universal game
of fish becoming man.

2

Llamas pray to the gods for snow. They chant
that it shall fall upon their artificial mount.
The llamas do not yearn
for tossed gumdrops or for popped corn.

Look,
even the great brown handsome official Kodiak
bear
has caramel in its hair.
Incomparable as he knows he is
the tough, tall golden lion looks at us
indifferent across
his molded hill, his helpful moat;
and, pregnant with a beast it ate,
the vicious, obvious and obscene
greedy-eyed old python
hauls itself along.

3

Gorillas lope and glare and crash
the glass in the Primate House.

The steaming place is packed
with folks who want to look
as at a wedding or a wake.
We advance. We retreat. We test. We wait.
We hope to see something masturbate.
We want to find a kind of King Kong
(magnificent but wrong)
caught and salted safe as us
behind the bars of flesh,
behind the glass of the face.

Twenty charming little tropical monkey kids
jabber in the phony trees. The gibbon is unkempt.
The yellow baboons bark, and they travel in groups.

There, ugly and alone,
awful and no longer young,
is that ornery thing
an orangutan.
Disconsolate, contrite,
red-haired widow who was once a wife
you pace and turn, and turn and pace
then sit on your repulsive ass
and with a hairy hand
and thumb delicately pinch an egg and
kiss its juice deep into your head.
Oh misery! Misery! You wretched bride.

Why only the silver monkey
glows and rests quietly,
nearly everything well,
a bit back in its tunnel
(which is lit
with its own created light).

This Primate House echoes
with our mixed cries;
it reeks with our ambiguous breath.
Each one caged as an oracle
I feel each upright animal
can tell
how much my life is a human life,
how much an animal death.

South Bend, April 1963

THREE MOVES

Three moves in six months and I remain
the same.
Two homes made two friends.
The third leaves me with myself again.
(We hardly speak.)
Here I am with tame ducks
and my neighbors' boats,
only this electric heat
against the April damp.
I have a friend named Frank—
The only one who ever dares to call
and ask me, "How's your soul?"
I hadn't thought about it for a while,
and was ashamed to say I didn't know.
I have no priest for now.
Who
will forgive me then. Will you?
Tame birds and my neighbors' boats.
The ducks honk about the floats . . .
They walk dead drunk onto the land and grounds,
iridescent blue and black and green and brown.
They live on swill
our aged houseboats spill.
But still they are beautiful.
Look! The duck with its unlikely beak
has stopped to pick
and pull
at the potted daffodil.
Then again they sway home
to dream
bright gardens of fish in the early night.
Oh these ducks are all right.

They will survive.
But I am sorry I do not often see them climb.
Poor sons-a-bitching ducks.
You're all fucked up.
What do you do that for?
Why don't you hover near the sun anymore?
Afraid you'll melt?
These foolish ducks lack a sense of guilt,
and so all their multi-thousand-mile range
is too short for the hope of change.

Seattle, April 1965

TWO PRELUDES FOR LA PUSH

I

Islands high as our inland hills
rise clean and sheer above the chill
April seas at La Push.
In a hush
of holy fog
the lean trees along their tops
(inaccessible to be climbed)
are offered up in flames of salt and wind.
And at La Push
the white, furious waves mass and rush
at each earthen island base.
These waves
are sudden, violent, unpredictable as grace.
They change White then
Blue then Green
swift as in Raphael's great wing!
I've seen it here where it has always hid:
Light, the shadow of our ancient God.

II

In the late afternoon light
even our human feet
start halos in the sand:
soft flashes of mind.
From the occult shore where you can see or feel
only a few shells
(shattered) among the lively stones,
we walk home.
I follow my younger brother,
for I am the visitor.

He knows the maze of fallen trees
that back up the blasted beach
for blocks: whether
this path or another.
Here the logs lie like lovers,
short by long, benign,
nudging gently in the tide.

Further up all the logs have died.
We walk through graves of wood
which are so oddly
borne out of the fecund sea,
each piece a last marker for itself,
each tomb planted with bulbs and whips of kelp.
Now as the water light fades,
I feel the monsters rage
again in this abandoned wood—gray
on darker gray.
Sometimes the flesh of the drifted face
is almost white! They seem to lift
their awful limbs,
broken from their lost hands.
Now the grotesque, giant shapes all
whirl awhile!
In the final light
the hard knots
of eyes scowl and brood
above the smaller dead
animals of wood.
I am afraid.
My brother walks ahead,
I reach for land:
the driftwood logs heavily shake
underfoot, and I awake,
balancing between my youth and my age.

THE PASS

Buttercups about the rocks and the sky
colored lupine lies

quiet in the brilliant grass
on the island by Deception Pass.

My young brother, his friends and I carefully
walk we

walk carefully along the edge
of the high flying bridge

and all look down
where gulls fall and rise over The Sound.

The awful height stirs in me
the huge, uneasy

gull
of my own soul.

I will not lean farther
over the bridge's sill with the others

(who can savor such a thrill). I will go back
and read the plaque

upon the rock.
But first I watch

a small, red speedboat hurry
beneath, pulling white, excited water flurries

like a living flag.
It passes a tug,

black and brown
(newly painted green

door) moving sure
as an old shepherd goes, before

a tremendous family of floating logs.
I wait until the tug's

completely underneath the span
(by then

even the wake of the younger boat is gone)
and turn

to walk back
alone toward the rock.

CARMEL: POINT LOBOS
(*for Thomas Sanchez*)

"It's called God," he said.
He is young and he had
walked or flown ahead
to the violent crag.
"When I see beauty like this
I want to die for it."—
Jump
to the far rock home
where the white, rolling foam
seethes,
rolls one eddy on another, and retreats
to lie still
in a momentary peace or pool.
A little way above and to the left, the gull
folks form
quiet lines of their own.
They wait along the brilliant height,
and then, when it's time,
fling them-
selves off into the wide
arcs and dips of their angelic suicides.
Against the overcast skies
their wings and bodies
weave
a gentle, shifting spiral figure
as of light—like the faster
nebulae of froth along the blue black water.
Suddenly the sun is out! and colors
brighten all about the iridescent Point
with its prehistoric birds and plants,

Santa Lucia rocks, its hints
of whales. Everything's more intense!
I feel afraid in this
shattering new light.
Dread drifts like fog around my heart.
Why? The sheer, terrible height?
Eerie glint and glance of mica in the rock
which catches in the glittering sea below?
The rough, long time ravaged coast
here and yonder, yonder,
yonder
far as you look? Or the unlikely cormorant
never so near or rare, so gaunt.
I see the seaside daisy
die so beautifully
here. It loses its nunlike coif
as the lavender leaves fall off
and tiny yellow rockets burst
about its heart
till only the perfect-
spiraled flower skull is left.
Last I touch
(as if with hope) the odd, succulent lettuce-
of-the-bluff.
Its gray-white rubber flower
leaves a chalk stuff on my finger
like a soft kind of death.
I feel stark
as this Point Lobos rock
where I sit and wait, older,
while you climb higher
among the hundred-million-year-old boulders
in search of the precious nest. I rise
in this beautiful place,

---

look about me like an anxious kid
or a hopeful god
and give what I have into the sea ahead.

BIG SUR: PARTINGTON COVE

the eyes of fire, the nostrils
of air, the mouth of water,
the beard of earth.
—WILLIAM BLAKE

1

We three park by the Big Sur Road
at Partington Cove,
disregard the furious note
(ALL TRESPASSERS WILL BE SHOT)
and begin the long, dancing trek
—I mean a zigzag walk—
toward the creek,
the tunnel and the Smuggler's Cave,
hoping to return somewhat more than alive.
In the light air of early June
transistor sounds rise and weave thin
from the stream
where we guess the guard catches fish, or swims.
I'm glad one of us knows the signs
to find the old tunnel.
A large, white half shell
hangs from a branch with a hole
in its middle
(which has been filled with metal),
and a little farther on
hangs
a stranger
omen woven of many-colored yarn
and shaped like a little kite.
The Indians say it is "God's eye."
Now with our shoes off

we soft slosh
across the creek,
toes a school of fish.
A brief, final
push
through the young brush
puts us at the aged tunnel.
The guard is safely ditched, we hope.
Short trip
through the moist dark
under artful, handhewn
timbers, and suddenly we are borne
out onto the brilliant cove
the thieves (and landscape) made a secret of.

2

Hidden as the middle of night
still this cove is bright
as day. The drop is immediate,
sheer to the shimmering sea,
and now you cannot get down
to the little half-moon
beach
bleached white. Blackbearded thieves
and smugglers
swagger.
Dressed in the ancient leather
they heave and hustle boxes there
and pour
out of a giant demijohn
of green
glass flashing in the sun.
They drink and sing.
They strip and swim

and huddle round the small fire
on the shore
in their human skin.
Then they dive away and are lost
into the glis-
tening eels of water weeds,
brown and supple as a leather whip.
Oh these are men that could make you weep!
We see the great, rusting iron hooks
in stone, and the broken links
of chains they used once to shinny up the rocks.

3

The risk is great around the cliff
beneath the cave of the thief. I almost twist
to my own death
stretched in the sea's long and stony bed,
where anemones lie lovely as an egg
and open up their mouths like downy chicks;
where poisoned thorns
pierce the purple flesh of urchins.
We single file about the hill's edge
and the pointed, dangerous piles
of rock. At last we climb
to the high, secret, hollow eye
of the cave and drop inside
where the smugglers hid
and stayed
like tears we never shed.

4

Anxious here, shivering, I find I need to love.
I am the father in the cave,

and I am drunk as Lot was in the shelter
made of skin the day he loved his daughter.
My sons squat in the dark together.
I know they will not hurt each other.
My mind heavily reels in time as I hover
on my haunch like an enormous bird.
And now I rise and stir to find
what I can for lunch—
or for our life in this long dark.
The belly of the cave is large!

5

We eat and sleep
and get up to bathe
in light at the mouth of the cave,
while one goes off to think
alone on a point of rock
over the smashing sea. I watch
from my place on the slab of stone
in the sun
beside, where I lie like a lover,
father or mother,
and look over
his naked hills at the black, wandering seas,
or I shift to watch the face
of the sky with its crags
and beards of clouds.
I see the slopes of his weathered head,
and all the tawny
hair along his body
blows
and lifts like shoots
of fern or grass.
Gulls jabber about his nests.

Eyes hold the little lives of the sea
in their pools of blue or gray.
The starfishes of his hands loll and soak
the sun on the rock,
and his foot
juts out
like a foot-
shaped cactus plant.
(I want to touch or catch
the glowing thing that lives in the cleft
at the root of the throat.)
Muscles of the belly
break like fields along this golden country!
For like the lost or stolen flesh of God,
the self, more alive or more dead,
opens on to the truth
of earth
and sea and sky—
and the thieves' cave yawns empty
of our smuggled body.

San Francisco, May 1967

LINES ON LOCKS
(or Jail and the Erie Canal)

1

Against the low, New York State
mountain background, a smokestack
sticks up
and gives out
its snakelike wisp.
Thin, stripped win-
ter birches pick up the vertical lines.
Last night we five watched the white,
painted upright bars of steel
in an ancient, New York jail
called Herkimer
(named for a general who lost an arm).
Cops threw us against the car.
Their marks grow gaudy
over me.
They burgeon beneath my clothes.
I know
I give my wound
too much thought and time.
Gallows loomed outside
our sorry solitary cells.
"You are in the oldest of our New York jails,"
they said.
"And we've been in books. It's here they had
one of Dreiser's characters arraigned."
The last one of our company to be hanged
we found
had chopped her husband
up and
fed him to the hungry swine.

They nudged the wan-
ing warmth of his flesh.
Each gave him a rooting touch,
translating his dregs
into the hopes of pigs.
And now with their spirited wish
and with his round, astonished face,
her changed soul
still floats about over their small
farm
near this little New York town.

2

The door bangs shut
in the absolute dark.
Toilets flush with a great force,
and I can hear the old, gentle drunk,
my neighbor in the tank,
hawk
his phlegm and fart.
In the early day
we line up easily as a cliché
for our bread and bowls of gruel.
We listen, timeless, for the courthouse bell,
play rummy the whole day long
and "shoot the moon,"
go to bed and jack off to calm down,
and scowl harshly, unmanned,
at those who were once our friends.
The prison of our skins
now rises outside
and drops in vertical lines
before our very eyes.

3

Outdoors again, now we can walk
to the Erie Locks
("Highest Lift Locks in the World!").
The old iron bridge has a good bed—
cobbles made of wood.
Things pass through this town everywhere
for it was built in opposite tiers.
Two levels of roads
on either side
the Canal, then two terraces of tracks
and higher ranks of beds: roads where trucks
lumber awkwardly above the town—
like those heavy golden cherubim
that try to wing about
in the old, Baroque church.
The little town—with its Gothic
brick
bank, Victorian homes with gingerbread frieze
and its blasted factories
(collapsed, roofs roll-
ing back from walls
like the lids of eyes)—
has died
and given up
its substance like a hollow duct,
smokestack or a pen
through which the living stuff flows on.

4

So we walk the long, dead-end track
along the shallow, frozen lake

where the canal forms a fork
(this time of year the locks don't work).
And now and again we look back,
for the troopers haunt the five of us
out the ledges toward The Locks.
(We know they want to hose
our bellies and our backs.
Or—as they said—
"Play the Mambo" on our heads.)
We do not yet feel
quite free—
though the blue and yellow, newly
painted posts
for ships
bloom gaily
in the cold, and the bulbs
about their bases bulge
for spring.
Soon the great, iron gates
will open out
and the first woman-shaped
ship,
mammoth, silent, will float toward
us like a god
come back
to make us feel only half afraid.
Until then,
though my friends will be gone
from this dry channel of snow and stone,
I'll stay here
among the monuments of sheer,
brown and gray rock
where you can read
the names of lovers, sailors and of kids

etched in chalk,
and in this winter air
still keep one hand over my aching ear.

Buffalo, March 1967

HELIAN
(after Georg Trakl)

The lonely times of the soul
It is lovely to walk in the sun
Along yellow walls of summer.
Our steps click lightly in the grass, but in the gray
Marble the son of Pan sleeps on forever.

Evenings on the terrace
We made ourselves drunk with tawny wine.
The peach glows red among the leaves.
A tender sonata . . . joyful laughter.

The silence of the night is beautiful.
In a dark meadow
We sometimes meet shepherds—and white stars.

When fall has come
A quiet brightness spreads in the wood.
Calmed we walk along the walls now red.
Our eyes grow round with the flight of birds.
At evening the white water sinks in burial urns.

Heaven has a holiday in naked branches.
In his clean hands the farmer carries bread and wine,
And the fruits ripen peacefully in the sunny room.

Ah, how solemn is the face of the beloved dead!
Still the soul takes delight in righteous vision.

    *   *   *

The silence of the wasted garden is powerful
As the young novice crowns his head with brown leaves
And his breath drinks icy gold.

His hands touch the age of bluish waters
Or touch the sisters' white cheeks in the cold night.

A walk past friendly rooms is like a lilting harmony.
Solitude—and the rustle of the maple tree,
Where perhaps the thrush still sings.

Man is beautiful. In the dark his self
Shines if he moves arms and legs, suddenly surprised,
While in their purple holes his eyes roll silently.

At the hour of vespers the stranger loses himself
In the black ruin of November—
Under decaying branches and along the leprous walls
Where formerly the holy brother went,
Sunk in the soft string music of his madness.

How lonesomely the evening wind dies,
And his head bends down
Dying in the dark of the olive tree.

*　*　*

The downfall of a generation is a staggering thing.
At such a time the eyes of the watcher
Fill with the gold of his stars.

In the evening the chimes die down
And do not ring anymore;
The black walls have collapsed in the square,
And the dead soldier calls us to prayer.

A wan angel (the son)
Walks into the empty house of his fathers.

The sisters have all gone away to the white old men.
The sleepwalker used to find them
Under the posts of the entrance hall at night,
Home from a sorrowful pilgrimage.

Their hair! How studded with filth and vermin!
He stands inside on his silver feet
As the dead sisters step out of the barren rooms.

Oh you psalms in the fiery midnight rain!
When servants strike the tender eyes with nettles
The childlike fruits of the elder tree
Bend down astonished over an empty grave.

The yellowed moons softly roll
Over the sick sheets of the young man
Before the winter's silence follows him.

* * *

A lofty destiny looks down on the Kidron River
Where the cedar, delicate creature,
Unfolds itself under the blue brows of the father,
And at night a shepherd drives his flock over the meadow.
Or there are cries in sleep
When a bronze angel comes up to the man in the grove
And the flesh of the saint melts on a glowing grate.

The purple vine creeps along the clay hut,
And bundles of yellow grain rustle.
The humming of bees. The flight of the crane.

In the evening those who have risen from the dead
Meet on the rocky paths.

Lepers look at themselves in the black waters
Or they open their garments flecked with filth,

Weeping, to the fragrant wind
Which blows from a rose-colored hill.

Slender girls grope through the lanes of the night
To find the loving shepherds.
On Saturdays gentle singing rings in the huts.

Let that song also tell of the boy,
Of his madness, of his white brow and of his going away—
Him whose flesh rots, as the eyes open bluish.
Oh how sad it is to meet again like this!

*   *   *

The grades of madness in black rooms.
Shadows of the old ones under the open door,
As Helian's soul gazes on itself in a rose-colored mirror,
And the snow of leprosy drops from his brow.

On all the walls the stars and the white
Shapes of light are put out.

Bones of the graves rise from
The silence of fallen crosses on the hill.
Sweetness of the incense in the purple night wind.

Oh you smashed eyes in black mouths,
When the grandson, gently deranged,
Meditates alone on the darker end,
And the silent God lowers his blue eyelids over him!

SEBASTIAN IN THE DREAM
(after Georg Trakl)

The mother carried her child in the white moonlight
In the shadow of the walnut tree and the ancient elder,
Drunk with the juice of poppy, with the lament of the thrush,
And silently,
With pity, a bearded face bent over them.

Gentle in the darkness of the window. All the old household goods
Of the fathers
Lay in ruin. Love and autumn's dreaming.

It was a dark day of the year in melancholy childhood
When the boy went down secretly to the cool waters,
To the silver fish, to peace—and a face!
His star came over him in the gray night
As he threw himself like a stone before black wild horses.

Or when he walked in the evening
Across the autumn graveyard of Saint Peter's
Holding his mother's icy hand—
In the dark of the burial house a fragile corpse lay silent
And the child opened his cold eyes over it.

But he was a small bird in barren branches.
The bell rang in nocturnal November.
Ah, the peace of the father when
He went down the winding, darkening stairs in his sleep.

2

The soul's tranquillity. A lonesome winter evening.
Dark figures of the shepherds by the old fish pond.

A little child in the hut of straw; how gently
The face falls with the black fever.
Holy night.

Or when the boy climbed silently up the gloomy Calvary Hill
Holding the hard hand of his father,
And in the dark crevices of rock
The blue shape of The Man passed through his own legend,
Blood flowed purple from the wound under the heart.
Very quietly the Cross grew up in his shadowy soul.

Love. In the black corners the snow melts.
A blue breath of air, caught brightly in the old elder,
In the shaded arch of the walnut tree: and a rose
Colored angel softly appeared to the boy.

Joy. When a sonata rang through the cool rooms at evening,
On the brown wooden beam
A blue butterfly crawled out of her silver cocoon.

Oh the nearness of death! Inside the stone wall
A yellow head bowed. The child was quiet
When the moon fell apart in March.

3

Glowing Easter bells in the grave of night
And the silver sounds of stars,
So in a shuddering fit
A dark madness dropped from the sleeper's face.

How quiet the walk down the blue river.
Thinking of what has been forgotten, while in the green branches
A thrush cries the ruin of an unknown thing.

Or when the boy walked in the evening by the fallen walls of the city
At the bony hand of the old man
Who carried a tiny, pink child in his black coat,
And the ghost of Evil appeared in the shadow of the walnut tree!

Groping across the green stairs of summer. How softly
The garden falls down in the brown silence of autumn;
The fragrance and the sadness of the old elder tree
When the silver voice of the angel died in Sebastian's shadow.

TWILIGHT LAND
(after Georg Trakl)

1

The moon stepped like a dead thing
Out of a blue cave,
And many flowers
Flutter all along the rocky path.
A sick thing weeps silver
By the pond of evening.
Over there the lovers
Died in a black boat.

Or the footsteps of Elis
Sound through the wood
Hyacinth-colored
And die away again
Under the oak.
Ah, the form of the young boy
Fashioned from crystal tears,
From shadows of the night.
Jagged flashes light up the forehead,
Which is forever cool,
And now on the hill just turning green
The echoing
Of the year's first thunderstorm.

2

So gentle are the green
Woods of our home,
The crystal wave
Dying along the broken wall—
And we wept in our sleep.

Now we stroll and linger
By the thorn hedge,
Singers in the summer night,
In the holy quiet
Of the distant, radiant vineyard.
The shadows of the cool castle
Of night are mourning eagles.
A moonbeam closes gently
The crimson wounds of grief.

3

You great cities of stone
Built on the plain!
Mute, his face dark,
The man who has no home
Follows the wind
And the barren trees on the hill.
Distant twilight floods!
The mighty, terrifying sunset glow
Is shuddering
In a mass of thunderheads.
Ah, you dying peoples!
A pale wave
Shattering on the night shore,
Falling stars.

THEY'VE BLOCKED EVERY WINDOW
(*after Tibor Tollas*)

Only this much light was left from our life:
The stars in the sky and a fistful of sunshine.
We watched for this day after day from the depths
Of the dim walls, every evening and every afternoon.
But they stole that too, our handful of sun:
They've blocked every window tight with tin.

I feel my eyes grow wide as I see the blue water
Of Naples. Above its shimmering shore
Vesuvius still waits, smoking—nearby
Are deeply suntanned, happy men. Do you see them?
But we live in darkness like the blind.
They've blocked every window tight with tin.

Ten of us lie smothering in a narrow hole.
Our ten mouths starve for air,
Gaping like the gills of fish
Driven to shore. We lack heart to breathe in,
Along with the stink, what would sustain.
They've blocked every window tight with tin.

The Alps send with their cool
West Wind sprays of the odor of pine
And your soul is rinsed by the purity of space overhead.
You can track the smell of snow to the smiling hills,
But yesterday my cell mate coughed up blood in pain.
They've blocked every window tight with tin.

The sound of whistles from pleasure boats shattering the silence, girls' laughter glancing off the walls,
No longer echo musically in our ears.

We do not hear the thousand reeds of summer's organ.
Our cells are deaf. Every sound is gone.
They've blocked every window tight with tin.

The warm voice of a dark, Barcelona woman,
Humming at twilight, filters through the
Distant gardens as she strums
Her guitar where dancers still color and dot the road.
But to our ears only the leaden days flow in.
They've blocked every window tight with tin.

We would probe for the velvet sky
But our fingertips drop with blood.
We are nailed up as in a coffin,
Only touched by burlap clothes or bugs.
We would stroke the beaming shoots of sun!
But they've blocked every window tight with tin.

At London dances in their silken dresses
Girls are gliding over the beautiful floors.
The bright down on their gentle hair
Glows in the graceful arcs of antique furniture.
The West is dancing! Maybe they have sold us then.
And they've blocked every window tight with tin.

Our tongues are awash for the fresh spice of spring
And we swallow drafts of swill, groaning.
Each stale, stinking sip would make your
Belly turn and spill.
Yet we suck every mouthful in.
They block every window tight with tin.

We gorge our starving guts on full
Dreams. The delicate taste of pastries
In Paris shops. Above their neon lights

I seem to see the silent terror creep.
And you will never again have dawn.
They will block every window tight with tin.

Let the radios howl hoarse about freedom
And the rights of men. It is here
That my self walled in—with millions more—
Feels the knot of Moscow's whip.
From Vach to Peking hear the prisoners moan.
If you are not careful throughout the world of men
They will block all the windows tight with tin.

PRISON POEM
(after Tibor Tollas)

A spider is sewing the silence;
He stitches up my shabby loneliness.
In the world I would not have seen you,
but here I greet you, fellow of my solitude.

First living thing I've seen for months!
I can talk to you!
Please look on me as a gigantic fly. Believe
I am caught in your web.

Suck my blood! What do I care?
I know. I know it is agony
to be hungry. But this is dinner for me—
to be able to give myself to you.

See, they appear through the air slowly:
Poison spiders with two legs.
When they bite me with the hate
in their eyes, or choke me in their iron snares,

I let them. Ejaculate all your poison!
A weight of fluid now protects me,
and the beauty in my heart moves toward the sun
though I am trapped by webs of stone.

THE OWL
(after János Hegedüs
and for Jill Bullitt)

The moon is in sight
On a poplar rotting in the night
Two lamps of eyes catch fire
Two clawed feet clutch at their desire
The profound owl
Ferocious and gray
Grotesquely feeds
For he is hungry as can be
He is hungry as can be.

HOMAGE TO RAINER MARIA RILKE
(for George and Finvola Drury)

I love the poor, weak words
which starve in daily use—
the ordinary ones.
With the brush of my breath
I color them. They brighten then
and grow almost gay.
They have never known
melody before who trem-
bling step into my song.

*　*　*

I remember my early poems.
In the silence of vine-covered ruins
I used to chant them to the night.
I linked them happily together
and dedicated them
as a gift for a blonde girl,
a fine golden chain of my poems.
But as a matter of fact
I was alone
And so I let them fall
and they rolled like beads of coral
spreading away in the night.

*　*　*

My mere desire shall reach
of itself into rhyme.
My ripe glance will softly burst
the stone coats of seeds

and my silence bring you ecstasy!
Wait! Someday the public
will drop to their knees
struck with my lances of light.
Like priests each will lift
the baroque chalice of his heart
out of his breast
and gladly give me blessing.

*   *   *

I am so young
I give myself to every sound.
My desire winds
its way
like the turnings of the garden
walk in the wind's beloved force.
I'll take up arms
at the call of any war.
From the coolness of this morning
at the shore
I will let the day lead
me next
toward the land-locked field.

*   *   *

At dusk, in the dark stone pines
I will let my shirt
fall like the lie it is
from my shoulders and back,
and pale and naked
plunge suddenly into the sun.
The surf is a feast
the waves have prepared for me.

Each one shakes like the last
about my young thighs.
How can I stand by myself?
I am afraid.
Still, the brightly joined billows weave
a wind for me
and I lift my hands into it.

*   *   *

O thou wakened wood amid the raw winter
you dare to show a brave sense of spring,
and drop your silver dross delicately
to show us how your yearning turns to green.
I don't know where I'm going,
but I will follow your needle paths
because the doors
I felt against your depths
before
are no longer there.

*   *   *

Put out my eyes! I will see you—
Close up my ears! I hear you still,
Without feet will go to you
and without a mouth will cry you.
Break off my arm!
I will take hold of you with my heart's hand:
Stop my heart! My brain
will beat—or ring my brain round with fire!
Still I carry you along my blood.

*   *   *

If it were quiet once—
if the casual and the probable
for once would cease their noise—
and the neighbors' laughter!
If the clamor of my senses
did not so much
disturb my long watch:
then in a thousandfold thought
I could think through to the very brink of you,
possess you for at least
the season of a smile,
and as one gives thanks
give you back again.

       *   *   *

This is the day when I reign
and mourn. This is my night.
I pray to God that sometime
I may lift my crown from my head.
For my reward may I not once
see its blue turquoise,
its diamonds and rubies
shivering into the eyes?
But perhaps the flash
is long since gone from the gem,
or maybe Grief, my companion,
robbed me. Or perhaps, in the crown
that I received there was no stone.

       *   *   *

Lord, it is time now,
for the summer has gone on

———————

and gone on.
Lay your shadow along the sun-
dial, and in the field
let the great wind blow free.
Command the last fruit
be ripe:
let it bow down the vine—
with perhaps two sun-warm days
more to force the last
sweetness in the heavy wine.

He who has no home
will not build one now.
He who is alone
will stay long
alone, will wake up,
read, write long letters,

and walk in the streets,
walk by in the
streets when the leaves blow.

April 23, 1967

THREE POEMS ON MORRIS GRAVES' PAINTINGS

1. *Bird on a Rock*

Poor, thick, white,
three-sided bird
on a rock
(with the big red beak)
you watch me sitting on the floor
like a worshiper
at your melancholy shrine.
All you can do is look. I mean
you lack any kind of wing or arm
with which to go home.
The three-toed foot of each odd limb
forms a kind of trapezium
about its edge
(though there is no web).
Oh bird, you are a beautiful kite
that does not go up.
You cannot even get down.
Because you've lost your mouth (it's gone)
only your great eyes still moan.
You are filled with the ancient grief,
fixed there lonely as a god or a thief.
Instead of limbs to bring you nearer
Morris Graves has given you
the sudden awful wings of a mirror!

2. *Spirit Bird*

Looking at Morris Graves' Spirit Bird
(1956), suddenly I
understood the structure of angels!
They're made of many colored streams

of the most intense, most pulsing light,
which is itself simply the track
of the seed of God across the void.
Each length of light seems to be a thread
that forms this angelic or spirit
stuff. But it's not. It's finer than that.
What gives the light its substance and shapes
the streams into the spirit thing
(apparent limbs and parts of body)
is the heavy, almost solid and
somehow magnetic *eyes* of angels.
These create the dark into which they glow,
and pull and bend about these sweeps of light.

3. *Moor Swan*

I'm the ugly, early
Moor Swan of Morris Graves.
I'm ungainly. I've got
black splotches on my back.
My neck's too long.
When I am dead and gone
think only of the beauty of my name.
Moor Swan   Moor Swan   Moor Swan.

THIRTEEN PRELUDES FOR PIONEER SQUARE

1. At the aged
Pittsburgh café under the street
(it's open only during the day)
the ragged pioneers get more meat
for their money.
A coat and tie gets hardly any.

2. Cigarettes die in
salmon tin
trays of gold and silver
and you pour your sugar
from a mason jar glint-
ing in the morning sun.

3. Moe's loan
keeps the pioneers in wine.
There's a trail of blood in the alley behind.

4. In the Florence Family Theatre
through the triple feature
the oldsters sit and cough.
Or they sleep it off
stretched across three seats:
they laugh and speak
loudly
out of their dreamed-up movie.
Some wake and go to the john,
where they solicit the young.

5. In the Six Fourteen the queers
think *they* are the pioneers.
When they dance they bleed and swallow

---

trying to decide who should lead
and who follow.

6. Next door the highly dressed men
with their highly dressed women
go
into the Blue Banjo.

7. Indifferent or reckless
(male and female)
two pioneers hail
and meet.
Near the street
in a stairway
they make it, their way.

8. One aged fellow, smashed
at a corner of the square
sits against the wall
(he doesn't stand)
and feeling the need
hauls it out and pees,
no longer a man.

9. The tall American totem
in this triangular square
scowls with its mask upon mask
at the Victorian shelter near.

10. The Square's mixed light
part-aged-gas, part-mercury unites
the drunk and beaten, swollen
Lady Indian
and beau a block from Brittania Bar,
the Negro weaving home from the B And R,

and the white man who can't
quite make it out
of the lounge at Rudy's Restaurant.

11. The great, garish,
painted concrete parking garage
fills in
across the street from the ancient building
where Bartleby worked and grew wary.
Its ruined lower halls have formed a marble quarry.
The upper floors are rich with pigeon shit,
and on a kitchen shelf still squats
the hunched up skeleton of a cat.

12. The oldest pioneer
still reigns not far from the Square
among tops, totem poles
on sale, little ash-tray toilet bowls,
lemon soap,
cups and knickknacks in the shop.
A real wooden Indian still stands
petrified at dying in the desert sand.
Six odd feet of bone
and tanned skin,
a purple cloth across his drained
loins (a little dry blood
is brown about the arrowhole above).
"Look Dad a real live dead
man," said a kid
and, tiptoe, tweaked
the king's mustache, which is red.

13. In the basements under the bars
about the Square
you can see bits of ancient stores

before the street was raised up in the air.
Pioneer Square
alone survived both water and fire.
Now the freeway named Aurora soars higher
and Seattle's ghost settle in another layer.

WHITE PASS SKI PATROL

His high-boned, young face is so brown
from the winter's sun,
the few brief lines in each green eye's
edge as of a leaf
that is not yet gone from the limb—
as of a nut which is gold or brown.

For he has become very strong
living on the slopes.
His belly and thighs are newly
lean from the thin skis.
Tough torso of the man, blue wooled.
Thin waist. White, tasseled cap of the child.

Beneath the fury of those great,
dark panes of glass, that
seem to take a man out of grace,
his gentle eyes wait.
(We feel their melancholy gaze
which is neither innocent nor wise.)

Like those knights of the winter snows—
with a healing pack
(sign of the cross on breast and back)—
serene, snow-lonely,
he patrols the beautiful peaks
and the pale wastes that slide like a beast.

Sometimes still blind from his patrol,
you'll see him pull down
from the dangerous Cascades his
heavy sledge of pain,

its odd, black-booted, canvas-laced
shape alive or dead, without a face.

Colors blooming in the sun, he
caroms down his own
path, speeds (bending knees), dances side
to side, balancing.
Under-skis glow golden in the
snow spume around his Christiana.

And as he lifts away from us,
skis dangle like the
outstretched limbs of a frog in spring.
He swings gently in
the air, vulnerable, so much
the "poor, bare, forked" human animal.

And now he slowly rises up
over trees and snow.
He begins to grow more thin, and then
vanishes in air!
as, high in the lithe boughs of pines,
the silver leaves flake silently down.

There are the shadow tracks he left
down the long, white hill
beside the lift. Wait! Look up! Cloud
trails in the bright sky!
Breathing a wake of snow ribbons,
something has just flown over the mountain!

Washington, February 19, 1966

HOMAGE TO HERMAN MELVILLE
(for Guenevere Minor Logan)

I

1

Yearning for the time, trembling with the hope of Isabel
(and then with the fear of her)
David came out of the woods above his sister's house
to begin a last, brief watch. It was early evening—
the end of the dark day's rain, and of his wandering.
He'd thought and wept and walked it seemed for weeks, ever since
Isabel told him who she was. And now he was resolved.
He'd leave his mother and his childhood home, his father's wealth.
And he would not marry Beth.
There was only one way left he could live with Isabel.
For he could not murder the memory of his father,
name Isabel his bastard sister. (Nor for that matter
hurt his mother so much.) Nor could he, with his long desire
to have a sister, ever give her up now he'd found her.
There was only one path. Thus he could not marry Beth.
Now David stood a moment at the skirt of the woods
in a faint road used only by dredges in the snow.
The trees formed an arch for fields sweeping down to the lake.
Scattered pasture elms seemed to shiver in the wet world.
The lake beyond was a sheet without a breath over it,
without the life to reflect even the littlest thing.
Only in the sun David knew the lake caught the quick,
green images that changed the blank
mirroring of a faceless heaven. On either side
the long mountain masses rose over the lake's farther shore,
their shoulders shaggy with hemlock and pine, the mien of the
mountains strange with a kind of aura or exhalation
in the dimming air. At their base black forests lay, and from
the owl-haunted depths of caves

and unused inland overgrowths of decaying wood,
odd intermittent moanings
came: rain shakings of trembling trees, underminings of rocks,
final crashes of great rotting limbs, and the devilish
gibberish of the forest ghost.
On the near shore (semicircular and scooped with fields)
the small farm home lay in the moist air, its ancient roof
a bed of bright moss, its north point, where the moss wind blows,
also soft with the furred growth—like the huge trunks in the groves.
A single shaft of vine waved up like a lightning rod
from a tangled web of plants
at one gabled end—against the other the dairy shed,
sides netted with Madeira vines. If you come close, perhaps
peeping through the lattice and the tracery of plants
that bar the tiny window,
you might see the mild captives, jugs of milk and the birch
white cheeses in a row, molds of gold butter, and the pans
of lily cream. In front of the house stood three immense
policing linden trees!
For a long way up they showed little foliage—almost to
the ridgepole of the house. But then, like three vast balloons,
suddenly their great, green, rounded cones float into the air.

2

On the rise over the house David waited the time
of Isabel. He felt more disembodied as the hour
grew near and shadows began to shoot slowly, deepening.
He tried to conjure the coming scene with his sister
as he told what must be done.
But fantasy failed, and only her face began to
appear to him (beautiful with the flesh of his father
whom David remembered from a beloved picture),
her face mixing with the shapes of air and crowding the air
away so that it was difficult for him to breathe.
The sweet form, buried in him since he had last seen her,

seemed to glide from a grave, fine hair sweeping far down her shroud.
Once just after they met he turned from her out of care,
began to leave, but she had caught his arms with her hands
and held him so convulsively her long hair swept side-
ways over him and half hid him.
"I'm so afraid," she said, "that the shadow of me will fall
over your whole life like these dark vines, dry tears of my hair."
But David had gently kissed her.
Now night shadows grew more thick, began to move to one black
and the place was nearly lost
under his feet as he circled down closer to the house,
only the three dim and hovering lindens leading him,
his mind serpentining like his path as he left the life
of his youth forever—and the rights of his birth. His walk
grew less quick when he saw the weak, single lamp in the house
struggle with the ancient day.
And then suddenly it was night. David was at the step.
Silence exuded from the small house till he stopped it
with his human knock. The light flickered and he heard the
creak of some inner thing in the room. David's heart shook
as he saw the outer latch
lifting near his touch, and—light in hand—Isabel was there
standing at the open half-door!
Nothing was said. There was no one near. David stepped, he
almost fell into the house,
and sat down pulling at Isabel's hand as if for life.
Quite faint he raised his eyes to her melancholy gaze.
Then, the fresh, rich sound of her voice played into the room,
slightly alien. She almost asked, almost stated,
"My brother . . . David." And she added, "But you seem so weak.
Am I a Gorgon blasting those who look? Wait. Rest here.
And I will bring you some wine."
"No," David said, "Don't leave. I'm weak for what I must say,
what we must do. But I have never been so strong. Please don't
take away your hand." He rose and caught her. Isabel's head

dropped against him and his whole form changed in the glossy light
of her long, ebony hair.
He felt a faint tremor in his arms, and with both hands
David parted the shadowed seas of the hair and looked
into her eyes, which were afraid.
She stopped shuddering, and the lovely eyes closed. It seemed
to David then that she was dead.
The deathlike beauty of her face! The death that leaves untouched
the latent calm and sweetness of the human countenance.
But now he felt her tremble again, and her eyes opened,
and she spoke. "David, I don't know what you mean, but your hope
is also mine. I will do what you want. For though I feel
an outer evil lowering
over us now, I know you will be careful with me."
David said, "My love touches yours.
Trust me, Isabel, in whatever strange thing I may ask.
Together, we will find the truth of our own life." Side
to side his eyes turned in his skull, but his voice stayed strong.
"And we will find our own glory."
Watching his face, she asked, "But is love cold and glory white?"
"It may be, for I believe to God that I am pure.
Let the world think what it will when we have made ourselves sure.
Listen!" David stood back from her. "This is what we want.
Do I not speak your own hidden heart, Isabel? Listen!
You know I cannot be an open brother to you,
for that would injure the memory both of us honor.
Yet if either of us left the other both would die.
Listen! There is only one way.
Let me hold you, and say." He gathered her to his arms
and she bent over toward him. His mouth wet her ear
as she felt his breath blow on her face, felt his whisper,
heard but could not believe the ancient words, "Be my wife."
Isabel did not move, except to fall closer, the thin
vines of her hair forming a kind of darkened arbor
over him, giving shape to the inarticulate,

suddenly intense love she felt.
All at once a terrible self-revelation shot
through David's mind. He kissed Isabel's mouth and he kissed her
hair and eyes again and again, his hands moving under
the black, delicate robe that dropped from her head.
One last change, and the two of them stood mute, coiled together
in the awful burst of light.

II

Toward sundown one night David stood in the Black Swan Inn,
the writing desk and blue-chintz-covered chest before him,
great brass lock glinting in the fire
he lit when he came in, to freshen the long closed room.
Fruitlessly his hands stirred through his pockets for the key.
How unlock the vision of his father—the picture
buried under bits of cloth
and other relics of his father's past. Combs. Portrait coins
of gold. David smashed the lock with an andiron. The lid sprang
open over his father's face
with its nameless, its ambiguous, unmoving smile.
It was David's first look at the loved face since he learned
his father's lust had got for him a bastard sister.
Now he swallowed with nausea, for he found certain lines
of Isabel's flesh glowing soft under the father's.
Painted before she was born, still the figure seemed to
level a finger at the air from which she had emerged.
David could not remember the lines of Isabel
from his memories of his dead father's face. Thus it was
the *picture* which now seemed to him to be her father.
Suddenly to David's eye
it quickened with an obscene life, and he hated it
with passion he felt full as his love of Isabel.
David lifted the portrait over his head as if to
smash it. His hands hovered there. But for now he turned the face

toward the wall and began to walk
about. He thought, "The picture shall not live. I've always kept
fragments and monuments of the past—a worshiper
of heirlooms, filer away of letters, locks of hair,
the thousand and more things love and memory make holy.
That's all over now. If any memory becomes
dear to me I'll not make a mummy of it again
for every passing beggar's spit and dust to gather on.
Oh, love's museum is foolish as the catacombs
where the laughing ape and abject lizard are embalmed
as if significant of some imagined charm—instead
of the decay and death of endless generations.
It makes of earth one awful mold.
And so much even for mementos of the sweetest!
As for the rest, I know now the twilight fact of death
first discloses (secretly) all ambiguities
of the departed thing. It casts
oblique hints and insinuates gross guesses never cleared.
By God, death should be the last scene of the last act of man.
The curtain inevitably falls upon a corpse.
Therefore I will never again play the vile pigmy
and by my small memorials
attempt to reverse the decrees of death. Let it all die
and mix again! There's no reason to keep this picture.
It must go—to keep my father's public memory
unviolated, because it tells the terrible truth
that is trying to drive me mad.
In the old Greek times before men's brains became enslaved
and their arms and legs, bleached and beaten in Baconian
factories, lost their barbaric tan and beauty—when the
round world was fresh and spicy as an apple (wilted now)—
in these old times our dead were not dished up like a turkey
in a trencher and set down with garnish in the ground
for the god-damned Cyclops to glutton on like cannibals!
Instead the friends who stay alive would cheat the anxious worm

and gloriously burn the corpse,
letting the spirit spread visibly up to heaven."
David stopped his pacing about.
He turned toward the small heap of embers still alive.
With his knife he slit the picture
clean, out of its faded gilt frame, dismembered the body
of the wood and laid the four lean pieces on the coals.
Soon the dry stuff caught the spark, and he rolled the canvas
into a scroll, tied it with a scrap of gold ribbon
from the trunk and committed it to the gathering flames.
Carefully he watched the first crispings and blackenings
of the painted tube. Suddenly unwinding from the burst
string, for one swift instant his father's freed face writhed up-
wards and stared at him, beseeching,
horrified. Then, shrouded in one broad sheet of oily fire,
the figure disappeared forever.
David darted his hands among the flames to rescue
the burning face, but had to draw them back, smoking and
turning black. Heedless, he crossed the room to the gaping chest,
scooped up old letters and other relics of paper
and threw them one after another onto the fire.
Shaking, David watched his private holocaust flame to ash,
putting an end to his paternity and to his past.
The future is an untraveled gulf.
There David stands, twice disinherited, his present self.

POEM, SLOW TO COME, ON THE DEATH OF CUMMINGS
(1894–1962)

"I care more about strawberries
than about death."

"Herr, es ist Zeit."

I

Lord, it is time now. The winter
has gone on and gone on.
Spring was brief.
Summer blasts the roots of trees and weeds
again, and you are dead
almost a year. I am sorry for my fear,
but you were father's age, and you were fond;
I saw it in your eyes when I put you on the plane.
Today it is too late to write
or visit as you asked.
I feel I let you die.
I chose the guilt over all the joy.
Now I know you cannot hear me say,
and so my elegy is for me.

II

I knew your serenity. Compassion.
Integrity. But I could not feel your death
until I visited your wife.
She is haggard with the burden of your loss.
I wish I had not come
before, when you were there,
and she served currant jam
on toast and you poured brandy in the tea

---

and laughed, slapping your thigh
and hopped, like a small, happy boy,
about your newly painted Village place.
Now the color on your walls and hers
is not fresh. It has peeled with the falling
of your flesh. Your paintings in the house already date,
especially the soft, romantic nude you did
(although I love it best):
Her dark hair full to hips,
girlish, unsucked breasts,
rather pensive belly, skin
a lucid gold or red like a faded blush.
Her beautiful, jet feminine bush.
And the limbs you made, thin with their own light,
with the glow of that other world:
Women. Estlin, your poems are full of love—
you wanted to know that other world
while you were still alive.
All poets do. All men. All gods.
Inside a girl we search for the lost wealth
of our self. Marcel says,
"Death is not a problem to be solved.
It is a mystery to be entered into."
Then you have what you wanted, Estlin,
for Death is a woman,
and there is no more need for a poem.
Your death fulfills and it is strong.
I wish I had not died when I was so young.

III

Your last summer at your farm
like a young man again you cut down
an aging, great New England oak.
Oh you are big and you would not start to stoop

even on that absolute day.
I feel you are a giant, tender gnome.
Like a child you came home
tired, and you called your wife
asking to be clean. Still tall you tossed
the odd body of your sweaty clothes
to her down, down the ancient stairs,
and it was there as the ghost
tumbled, suddenly you were struck
brilliant to your knees! Your back
bent. You wrapped your lean,
linen arms close around your life
naked as before our birth,
and began to weave away from earth
uttering with a huge, awkward, torn cry
the terrible, final poetry.

July 1963–August 1964

ON THE DEATH OF KEATS:

(Lines for those who drown twice)
(for John Alioto)

—*I am recommended not even to read poetry,*
much less to write it. I wish I had
even a little hope.

—*Send me just the words "good night,"*
to put under my pillow.
KEATS TO FANNY BRAWNE

—*I do not care a straw for foreign flowers.*
The simple flowers of our spring are
what I want to see again.
KEATS TO JAMES RICE

I

The last month in your little Roman house
your eyes grew huge and bright as those
a gentle animal opens to the night.
Although you could not write or read
you were calmed by the thought of books
beside your bed.
(Jeremy Taylor your favorite one.
Plato and the comic Don.)
"How long is this posthumous life of mine
to last," you said.
What is a poet without breath enough?
The doctor made you swallow cupfuls of your blood
when it came up
out of your rotten lungs again.
Your study of medicine
made you suffer more the movements
of your death. One tiny fish

and a piece of black bread
to control the blood
every day you died. You starved for food
and air. For poetry. For love.
(Yet you could not read her
letters for the pain.)
One night you saw a candle flame
beautifully pass across a thread from one
taper to start another.
All month you heard the sound of water
weeping in the Bernini fount.
You asked your friend to lift you up,
and died so quietly he thought you slept.
They buried you with Shelley
at a cold February dawning
beside his drowned heart
which had survived a life
and death of burning.

II

Ruth and I visited your grave
in Rome's furious August rain.
The little old Protestant plot
beyond the pyramid the Romans, home from Egypt, made
in the middle of the city.
All the names are English,
which nobody knows or nods to
in the awful noise and light. Nobody speaks.
This rain springs from ancient seas
that burst
behind the bones of my face
and wash in salt tides
over the small shells of my eyes.
Since my birth

I've waited for the terror of this place.
The gravekeeper in his hooded black
rubber cloak
wades ahead of us toward your tomb.
The streams that shape and change
along the tender's rubber back
light in the thunder flash
into grotesque slits of eyes.
They see my fright. Ruth's hand
is cold in my cold hand.
You, Keats, and Shelley and Ruth
and I all drown again
away from home
in this absurd rain of Rome,
as you once drowned in your own phlegm,
and I in my poem. I am afraid.
The gravekeeper waits.
He raises his black arm.
He gestures in the black rain. The sky
moans long.
His hooded eyes fire again!
Suddenly I can read the stone
which publishes your final line:
Its date is the birthday of my brother!
"Here lies one whose name was writ on water."
Oh Keats, the violet. The violet. The violet
was your favorite flower.

ELEGY FOR THE REV. MR. JAMES B. HODGSON
(1892–1963)

I haven't talked to you since your death
but your picture still breathes
and flames in my dreams and at my eye.
I can tell you as a boy
folding back and back the loam
of your family's farm
as the beginning morning light grows like grain
in Yorkshire or as wind-blown fur
changes texture—
while your mother
turns again the parti-colored
fields of quilts along the beds
and furiously sweeps your little room.
Or see you following the great, slow team
while you memorize the paradigms
of Greek
you pasted on the wooden wagon seat.

As a man you shepherded a white
Presbyterian church, pointed and at rest,
a unicorn among the Iowa farms,
penned beside a field of marble colored blooms.
But I will surely not forget
that you also taught.
Small, lean body, annular face and eyes, metal rims
and a fixed (false teeth) grin
make up the picture
of my first beautiful teacher.
You taught us to listen to a book
like a lost, ancient father's talk,
and from the light in your eyes we knew

you
would become aroused
if a handsome library passed.
You gave me Goethe's *Faust* in German
and together we struggled over "time" in Bergson.
(Still for some instruction you were not so strong—
walked away from a film on sex for the young.)
And you paid
the favorite praise to my poems when you said,
small eyes gray with peace,
"You have experienced deeply both of nature and of grace."

I left the school, tried my young luck.
But I kept coming back
as if to beg someone's pardon.
Your wife made lunch in the garden
while you caressed the flower beds,
patting the dirt and pulling weeds—
or talked of your son studying abroad,
of your wife's portrait paintings on the wall,
and of your own apocalyptic book—undone until you would "retire
and have the time."
Twice I stayed the night.
But you would never break
reserve, and said at last,
"I shall follow your career with interest."

Sixty-five came, and you bought a tiny farm
where you turned
your father's earth over in your hand
and cherished close your aging wife.
But she gave up her life
the very first, quiet year,
and you would not stay there
by yourself, nor finish up your work.

Soon you too took sick
and died—with your mouth and cheek
all caved in like a hill of earth
under the heavy disc of a stroke,
unable to talk.

Still it isn't this I remembered on the afternoon
I learned your final lesson.
I was filled with an ancient image
seated on the stage
as you waited to speak at school.
You seemed to curl
forward into a ball;
your heavy head fell,
hands were born farther down between the knees
as an infant is
before he leaves his early night.
You seemed to become more taut,
more formal
or compact, more integral.
And as the mass of your body bent,
and folded some, I saw it give off bright
streams as of language or light!

THE WEEPING
(for Thomas Morgan 1873–1948)

Why do I still run
from the grandfather in my dream

I thought my love for him
died when I was young

Oh Grandfather you are alive
in the huge houses of my inner eye

Like the sudden yellow gleam
in the windows of your farm

When we come around the turn
and in the summer sun your high ancient home

Looms on the hill
I remember you cried like a young girl

Standing by the well
after Grandmother's funeral

Your mountainous beautiful
Welsh face all filled

And the roots of your hands still
Grandfather you blessed me once when I was ill

In my dream it was you who died
as I thought you did

And it was I who cried
as I never would.

November 12, 1963

GRANDMOTHER DEAD IN THE AEROPLANE
(for Abigail E. Logan 1875–1968)

Grandmother after that late eclipse
when I lay drunk in the weak, April grass
and watched the moon on the last, best Friday night
grow awful and cruel and then lean
slowly out of the light
(become an odd, dark rock
under which some of us
still have our moving lives) —
after that you can hold the very first
of your favorite Easters.
At least a good and gaudy card
came each year before you died.
There is no message yet this time.
Instead I feel you addressed
and mailed *me* on this Saturday plane.
Grandmother you have verified the myth
inside my head. . . . Inside my head
I carry your gentle, senile hunch-
back and your swollen ankles
still shuffle here in the airplane's halls.
Your rheumy, red old eyes leak out all our tears.
Look out, Grandmother!
Or else I will look in. The plane
window angles near us (well, between)
and your face
reflects. You are spread
thin and shiny over all this Holy Saturday.
Grandmother is there ever any Easter
without a hope? And will the moon
be light

for the Saturday dance again tonight?
I am angry since you've died.
The 727 motor at my ear
is joining me fast to Detroit
on my Easter trip,
and it has quite
disoriented my small, waning life.
Everything has died.
I'll learn how to mourn quite mad
if never to rave in love.
I want to stay up here forever,
Grandmother. For I am tired of the fogged earth
down there
with its esoteric itch of flesh.
"Time Flies." I swear my soul has just turned
ninety too. On the night I visited
and stayed
in your sad, old ladies' home
I really shook. Sick, I shivered
from the barbed, tiny animals of dread.
I kissed you and I cried
and tried to sleep
in the ancient woman's bed
(your absent friend) —
her family plastered to the wall.
something flickered back
and forth in me, black and white,
and I touched myself heavily
again and again
to see if the young
man (I was twenty then) was anywhere around.
Oh you and I too have had our scenes,
since I was the chosen one.
When I was ten

and you visited the farm
you unwrapped your long,
red, lacy velvet doll
and then undid the bones
of china for its tiny house.
You took the picture albums
out of the attic trunk. And took that
milky, moonshaped paperweight.
We squatted crosslegged on the attic planks
and swayed and wept for what
you made me think
the two of us had lost.
Was it really only you
who were not young
and who no longer had a home?
Oh, I did love you my ardent old Mom.
It was the second time for me,
my first mother gone.
You pushed me proudly in my pram,
and I remember this:
right in front of your friends
I wet my pants
until I knew you noticed me.
You fixed the rockers on my broken horse.
And just before the picnic once
put a poultice on my swelling thumb
to draw the sliver out.
Now I watch the nail's moon
blacken by my pen.
Look. My plane has never gone
far: it hovers in your air.
Christ what am I doing here?
Communing with you I guess.
Well then, come on,
my beloved crone. Open up.

Now I lay me down
in your aged lap and sleep
clean through this Easter.

Easter, 1968

LINES FOR A YOUNG MAN WHO TALKED

But I wish you would not hang your head.
It is that image lags inside my mind.
If you had known how much we need
to help our friend (Oh I think in some old
innocence perhaps you did),
you would not hang your head.
It was out of your own gentleness you cried
for aid. And it's not because I'm fond
of you (although I am) as if you were my son instead
of my young student and my young friend
that I do not want you to hang your head.
It is this: the bit you told—
no, not *what* but simply *that* you said—
was like a gift! An ancient gift of horses or of gold.
It was a grace. Oh I suppose you thought you had confessed.
But I am not a priest. To say you had been bad
and young and let you hang your head.
Use me to find in what way you are good.
Christ, listen to your own charitable word!
We spoke so that you might understand
and be merciful to yourself. Here, give me your hand
for it is I who must feel ashamed
again, until you do not hang your head.

South Bend, April 1963

THE RESCUE

(for Roger Aplon and James Brunot)

I doubt if you knew,
my two friends,
that day the tips
of the boats' white wings
trembled over the capped,
brilliant lake
and fireboats at the regatta
rocketed their giant streams
blue and white and green
in the sun just off the shore,
that I was dying there.

Young jets were play-
ing over the lake,
climbing and falling back
with a quick, metallic sheen
(weightless as I am
if I dream),
sound coming after the shine.
They rose and ran and
paused and almost touched
except for one
which seemed to hang back in the air
as if from fear.

I doubt if you know,
my two beloved friends—
you with the furious black beard
your classical head
bobbing bodiless above the waves
like some just appearing god

or you, brown, lean, your bright
face also of another kind
disembodied
when you walked upon your hands—

That as you reached for me
(both) and helped my graying bulk
up out of the lake
after I wandered out too far
and battered weak along the pier,
it was my self you hauled
back from my despair.

SUZANNE

You make us want to stay alive, Suzanne,
The way you turn

your blonde head.
The way you curve your slim hand

toward your breast.
When you drew your legs

up, sitting by the fire,
and let your bronze hair

stream about your knees
I could see the grief

of the girl in your eyes.
It touched the high,

formal bones of your face.
Once I heard it in your lovely voice

when you sang—
the terrible time of being young.

Yet you bring us joy with your
self, Suzanne, wherever you are.

And once, although I wasn't here,
you left three roses on my stair.

One party night when you were high
you fled barefoot down the hall,

the fountain of your laughter
showering through the air.

"Chartreuse," you chanted
(the liqueur you always wanted),

"I have yellow chartreuse hair!"
Oh it was a great affair.

You were the most exciting person there.
Yesterday when I wasn't here

again,
you brought a blue, porcelain

egg to me—
colored beautifully

for the Russian Easter.
Since then, I have wanted to be your lover,

But I have only touched your shoulder
and let my fingers brush your hair,

because you left three roses on my stair.

LOVE POEM

Last night you would not come,
and you have been gone so long.
I yearn to find you in my aging, earthen arms
again (your alchemy can change my clay to skin).
I long to turn and watch again
from my half-hidden place
the lost, beautiful slopes and fallings of your face,
the black, rich leaf of each eyelash,
fresh, beach-brightened stones of your teeth.
I want to listen as you breathe yourself to sleep
(for by our human art we mime
the sleeper till we dream).
I want to smell the dark
herb gardens of your hair—touch the thin shock
that drifts over your high brow when
you rinse it clean,
for it is so fine.
I want to hear the light,
long wind of your sigh.
But again tonight I know you will not come.
I will never feel again
your gentle, sleeping calm
from which I took
so much strength, so much of my human heart.
Because the last time
I reached to you
as you sat upon the bed
and talked, you caught both my hands
in yours and crossed them gently on my breast.
I died mimicking the dead.

ON THE HOUSE OF A FRIEND
(for Robert Sund)

Under the lightly leaved
April trees,
your small red house seems to speak—
mildly. It lets you come down
into it from the easy sloping lawn.
Your house is very clean,
for each room
has been well swept by your young friends.
You gave up your bed to them
because they are in love: the lean,
glad girl with long hands
who shares easily all she has
with her blond, gentle boy.
It is this the house seems to say
at the Dutch, open half-door:
their love and yours.
Look, a hapless slug
suns and glows on the madroña stump
beside the porch. So slow, so
slowly it goes
toward the great, full mushroom
resting there. That home
shall keep him from harm.
Beside the rhododendrons in the yard,
your red, Iceland
daisies make a light sound.
Their music seems to change and go
between the flowers and the glass in the window.
Robert, now this small
red house (as in a child's
book) smiles
with the smile of your own face.

LINES FOR MICHAEL IN THE PICTURE

There is a sense in which darkness
has more of God than light has.
He dwells in the thick dark.
—F. W. ROBERTSON

I

You are my shadow in the picture.
Once I thought you were my brother,
but to be honest, he and I were never friends.
(Even our boyhood secrets never brought us closer.)
Odd the way you stand behind and to the side,
like a shade. Still it is your own
darknesses you stay in.
You generate shadow like a light
or like an odor
falling from your arrogant shoulder,
eddying into your eyes.
The great eyes almost seem to glaze.
Look! They seem to tip!
Your eyes are alive with the gestures of death.
You've got something of mine shut in there, Michael.
I must enlarge the picture
and let it out
of your ancient, melancholy face.
My shadow yearns for peace.

II

You came to my house
just separated from your life,
your clothes still burning in the chimney
(fires tended by furious women),

books piled or bent ("She has made
me stupid," you said)
or lost. Dishes in boxes, smashed.
Pieces of your life gaped from paper sacks.
Shelves were stripped like flesh,
letters from your friends destroyed—
family scowling, all utterly annoyed.
Who was to blame?
Your marriage already gone
at twenty-one,
you said, "I have abandoned myself," and wept.

III

Something binds every kind of orphan.
I could find my own loneliness in your face,
hear it in your voice.
But there is something else,
some lost part of myself I seem to track
(did you know I used to be called Jack?),
so I follow like a blind animal
with hope (and with fear)
your brilliant, shadow spoor.

IV

I followed in the sun
until we reached the silent pine
the day we climbed the mountain.
We were with your friends, Marie, Jim.
I was jealous of them
for they had known you longer.
It was then I began to wish
you were my brother. We cut
some sticks and walked behind.

103

Suddenly the pied fields, farms
and iridescent waters of The Sound
blue or black
simply fell away from where we watched
like the holdings of a haughty god,
and from the mountain top
I found an island in a lake
on the other island where we stood.
That is the way you seem,
there is your home.
Your eyes are like the inwardmost island
of that inwardmost lake,
and your tears are the springs of that.
Ah well, we all weep, Michael.
One of our eyes cannot even know the other
(except, perhaps, with a picture)

V

Down the mountain again
we stopped to swim
in a cove of The Sound—the water
actual ebony beside the brilliant sky.
You walked away from the rest
for you had seen
another hill you hoped to scale
rising down into the sea.
Marie sat on the steps behind
as we undressed.
(She wouldn't swim with us.)
Tall, classical, you poised at your own place
on the stones black from the wet
of waves, and dove suddenly
into the heartcold sea.
And for a silent while

you were gone with no sign,
the time of a cold change.
Coming back you brought up
a part of the dark
of the seas in your eyes
and some of the blue, obscure snow of the hill
drifted on your thighs and arms
in the shattering sun.
Jim and I dunked briefly,
chattering and quickly pimpled.
We carefully kept our backs
to Marie as we dressed. You
simply stood, naked and plumed,
half hard
on the bridge of the rock
and (almost as an afterthought) turned
toward the steps.
Marie looked easily at your body
and smiled. You grinned
and climbed toward your clothes.
Suddenly I felt that she
had watched the dark
rich-haired shadow of me.

VI

You and I, Marie and Jim
that night on the island shore
piled up log
on log on log (we couldn't stop)
and built a driftwood fire so big
I think it scared the four of us
into dancing barefoot on the sand.
The greatest fire we'd ever seen!
We didn't join our hands,

but the eyes of flames
grew huge
and struck us blue,
then red. Blue. Then yellow.
Blue. And as we danced and danced higher
the freshly made fire
threw our shadows each on each
and blurred us into a family
sometimes three, sometimes four
close as lovers on the beach!

VII

It was the last ember
of that transforming island fire
that seems to fade in your eyes in the picture.
It makes you brother, friend, son, father.
If it isn't death, it is change,
and in that fine shadow flame
what was locked is yours, Michael, as much as mine.

Seattle, May 1965

SAN FRANCISCO POEM

"A pier," Stephen said. "Yes,
a disappointed bridge."
   —JAMES JOYCE

1

We moved like fingers
over the curved arms of the rock
pier at Aquatic Park,
saw the black-
haired, half-stripped boy haul back
from the sea the huge, live hand
of a crab. It charmed
and scared a playing kid.
"O-o-o-oh," she said
and jumped
right straight up
in the air,
where she changed
into a low, light limbed star.

2

And where we walked
in that watery park
the formally
happy families
fished on the pier.
From his one good eye a floored flounder
gazed with long despair,
and the dogfish shark
writhed on the concrete walk—
shucked aside

by the female touch of time.
Half-dissected by a gull
he bleeds his tears of oil.

3

Purple flowers shadowed the island prison
(windows closer than I had ever seen)
The small harbor freight train screamed
along the sand
across
from the curved pier, across
from us.
Its racket shook the ancient circus
sprawling in the sun:
the bursting muscle man,
a lovely, light-haired gamin
of a girl in blue (and little else)
whose breasts were never false
to man;
it nudged a midget growing like a stalk of corn;
an old salt who blends
with the sand, living out of sacks,
purple bats
and mothers inked along his back,
once-bright snakes
dying in the heat blackened
flesh of his aged arms.
(And other oldsters roll
their bocce ball
about the nearby green.)
When they hear the train
stark-naked kids all pause in their paradigms.
The little girls tell the little boys.
Gulls wheel about the dinging buoys.

4

At last we walk
to the far end of the break-
water pier, which turns
so gen-
tly in the sun
of the long, April afternoon.
There is some grotesque, giant thing
still there
left behind by a war
(or a very melancholy sculptor).
At the circular edge
of this stone stage
I can hear the little herds of fish
be still, or stir and shift to graze
on the sea's beautiful grass.
The pied, ambitious ducks dive
and are gone away
(long or shorter as the case may be)
under the mild surface of the bay.
One sleek,
brown-and-black duck
suddenly comes back
with a meal quivering in its beak.
Another dives and appears,
dives and reappears,
still poised but quite pissed
off at the absence of a fish.
The few colorful birds
(absorbed)
dive and dot
the black,
shimmering canvas, alive, abstract.

5

You and I sit on the concrete bench
at pier's end and watch—
each
other and the far folks upon the beach.
They watch you as you take a leak
with no attempt to hide.
We read Roethke's "Words for the Wind,"
smile at the faggot with the fat behind,
admire together
a white, three-masted schooner,
and read the signs that tell us where
we are.
"Ghiradelli Square." "Drink Hamm's Beer."
"Cable Crossing. Do not anchor here."
Because the concrete spot
where I sit
suddenly grows too hard
(and because I am really tired)
I tuck the body of your coat under my head,
curl up on my arm
and fall easily into a dream:
Two people surface and begin to swim.

San Francisco, April 1966

LINES FOR A FRIEND WHO LEFT

"Ich starre, wie des Steins
Inneres starrt."
—R. M. RILKE

Something vague waxes or wanes.
I have been grieving since you've gone,
and I am stark as the heart of the stone.
I have this grief because you are a ghost
and a thief. Since you left I have missed
my own self. For your absence
steals my presence.
Next I lose my dignity. At night
I put on the dirty shirt
and coat you left
and go out
to hunt for you in the bar or street
feeling your private warmth. Last night
I thought I saw your very face
(voice of another)
in the place of a folk singer.
(The heavy mouth almost seemed to sneer
at the end. I could not be sure.)
I have not heard
since you've gone, so I still yearn
for any sign
of your life. For if you died
I did too. I
Can no longer quite
make out your body's breadth and height,
and there is something vague that grows in me
like a dead child.

Write
or come back, before I forget
what we both look like.

LETTER TO A YOUNG FATHER IN EXILE

When I last wrote
I was so hung up with old guilt
or fright
       I could not think
what *you* might need—you who are
caught by this fucking war
in another land,
gone from parent, from calming scene, friend,
who had to leave school just as that
began to help
              shape
the keen blessing of your insight,
which is bright and quick
with presence as a fresh, dawn-white
drop of milk.
          And now you have a son
whom you are also exiled from
double-walled away
             by
both an outer and the terrible inner fight
(more bloody than any human battle yet,
Rimbaud said).
Sweat, tears and sperm
press together from the muscles of a man
such as you are in our time—
an age which is only made
(it seems) for the old
who dare to send
               their gifted young
off to the predicted geld-
ing of a war, or jail, or to some other land

from which as you they never can
come back.
So you've become a lumberjack—
and undertake
the most dangerous of lumber jobs
choking, hooking, lassoing logs,
risking your young arms and legs
because you are not afraid.
Better to take the lives of bears and trees
than any of those
you feel inside yourself or in the eyes
of brothers, or in your own
yet unseen son's
                    burgeoning flesh.
He learns to nurse—
a sharp and tender boy
we have the hope to say—
and grows out guts, limbs:
desires to return what his mother gives.

Next, as do all kids, I guess,
he will try to learn to piss
with all the strength of giants, Gulliver
and Pantagruel, heroes who could stop a war
alone, or Leopold Bloom, higher
than two hundred fellow scholars
against the white wall
of his elementary school.
(Or the young man in Freud's dream
whose powerful river could rinse clean,
as in a famous, ancient marvel,
the filthy Augean stable.)
And one day your son will learn to swim and ski

with your own passing grace and beauty.
And perhaps in a heavy, red
woolen sweater and a massive, black beard
he will hunt swift and kill (as you) the lithe
heavy bear, and pose squatting alongside
its great, steaming, brownfelled thigh.
Michael, your son's rifle will resound
and resound
though you may only see his young kind
and not himself,
since you are banned, and since you do not have
his mother for your wife.
And you have lost one daughter or son
already, under
the murdering stress
of our own human hopelessness.
After the tender pulsing in
of your full tide of semen,
with the clouded image of a son
(which always brightens when we come)
once there
was the fusing of the sea and shore—
meeting of another half
                              life
to carry yours.
But then war
on the womb, solid hits—
and death for the quick new part
of you and her.
And now again the grotesque hidden scars
that form and grow in all our hidden wars.
With this slow grief and your present loss of roots,
with all your unwritten books
and your rock hard, exiled life

(its vicious, black, summer logging flies):
Jesus, how in hell do you survive!

And finally this, my own thoughtless role:
you write me a note
                        about your first son,
a bastard like the rare and brilliant one
of St. Augustine,
and in my brief reply I do not even
mention
                    him. Well, I see (sadly) I am cruel.
And I too know how to kill!
For when I last wrote
and said I wanted to forget
                                (abort
your image out of my mind)
simply because you are not around
for my solace and my life, now
I see I raised what came
                            into my hand
against you. Thus
I am loving and as treacherous
as parent or as child—in the black
ancient figure you and he may fight to break.
Oh my lost, abandoned brother,
you know you had a father.
Now let your son
say so with the jets of milk
his drawn from yours
and from the breasts of a mother,
whose fecund spurts
of white
as in the Tintoretto work
where young Hercules is nursed

by a god—have formed the brilliant wash
and brush
of stars across the dark, inner wall
of our still radiant, woman world.

Buffalo, December 1968

THE SEARCH

But for whom do I look?
The whole long night you will see me walk
or maybe during the day
watch me pass by.
But I do not wander—
It is a search. For I stop here,
or here, wherever people gather.
Depot, restaurant, bar.
But whom do I seek?
You will see me coming back
perhaps at dawn. Sometimes
the faces seem like tombs.
I have tried to read the names
so long my eyes darken in their graves
of bone. (The bodies of our eyes
lie side by side
and do not touch.)
But for whom do I look? My search
is not for wife, daughter or for son
for time to time
it has taken me from them.
Or has wrenched me from my friend:
I will abruptly leave him,
and I do not go home.
For whom do I seek? Out of what fear?
It is not for queers,
for my search leads me from their bars.
It is not for whores,
since I reject their wares,
or another time may not.
Then for whom do I look?
When I was young I thought

I wanted (yearned for) older age.
Now I think I hunt with so much rage
that I will risk or lose
family or friends for the ghost of my youth.
Thus I do not know for what I look.
Father? Mother?
The father who will be the mother?
Sister who will be the brother?
Often I hunt in the families of others—
until hope scatters.
I will call up friend or student at night
or I will fly
to see them—will bask and heal in the warm
places of their homes.
And I must not be alone
no matter what needs be done,
for then my search is ended.
So now the panicked thumbs of my poem pick
through the grill. They poke
the lock
and put out a hand and then an arm.
The limbs of my poems
come within your reach.
Perhaps it is you whom I seek.

NOTES

1) I grouped these poems on the basis of person and address. Sections 1 and 3 are made up of pieces addressed primarily to a general audience where the speaker uses the first person (1) or not (3). The poems of Sections 4 and 5 are addressed secondarily to a general audience but primarily to given persons whether living (5) or not (4). (The speaker uses first person throughout these latter two sections.) The pieces in Section 2 are all translations mixed in person and address—except for the Morris Graves poems which however are derivative in another way. Poems are roughly chronological in the order of each section.

2) "The Pass," "Thirteen Preludes . . ." "White Pass Ski Patrol," "On The House of a Friend," and "Lines for Michael . . ." were written in Washington State except for the latter which however was begun there and which cites places there: Mount Erie on Whidbey Island and beaches on that island and at La Conner. Deception Pass is a waterway betwen Whidbey and Fidalgo islands. La Push is an Indian community on the Olympic Peninsula. Pioneer Square is the oldest section of downtown Seattle, and White Pass is a ski resort in the Cascades.

"San Francisco Poem" names the aquatic pier in the marina there. Point Lobos extends into the sea near Carmel, California, and Partington Cove is in the Big Sur area near the Hot Springs, California.

"Lines on Locks" speaks of Herkimer near the Erie Canal in eastern New York State and thus blurs that town with Little Falls (not named) just to the east. "The Zoo" is Brookfield Zoo in Chicago and "The Rescue" was staged on the shore of Lake Michigan in that city.

3) "Homage to Herman Melville" is based closely on scenes from Melville's *Pierre,* while "Homage to Rainer Maria Rilke" is based

on fragments and in some cases on complete poems from several of Rilke's books. One such complete poem is *Herbsttag"* which concludes my "Homage" and which also figures briefly in ". . . on the Death of Cummings" in the epigraph to that poem. The translation of *"Herbsttag"* was published in an earlier version dedicated to Paul Carroll in the old "Chicago Magazine." The Rilke epigraph to "Lines for a Young Man Who Left" is from his *Das Marien-Leben.*

4) I am grateful to several people involved in the translations: James Wright suggested I choose the three Trakl poems included here, *"Helian," "Sebastian im Traum"* and *"Abendland."* Their translations in earlier versions were commissioned by The Bollingen Foundation with the help of Elizabeth Kray at the YMHA Poetry Center. Mrs. Stephen Rogers (in particular), Robert Bly, and Max A. Wickert at one time or another swelled my small German.

The translations from the Hungarian poets were undertaken at the urging of David Ray and were included in *From the Hungarian Revolution,* which he edited for Cornell University Press. Since I know no Hungarian my work was done from German translations and from literal Englishings by Watson Kirkconnell.

5) The three Morris Graves paintings which I used I saw in a Graves show at the Seattle Art Museum in 1966, and they are owned by collectors in the Seattle area. The Seattle Art Museum owns "Moor Swan."

6) If Morris Graves is my favorite older American painter, Jim Johnson is my favorite younger one, and I dedicated the Big Sur poem to him and his wife because early paintings of his first conveyed to me concretely the concept of the rapport between landscape and the human body which that poem uses.

Like Blake in his *Prophetic Books* (Epigraph to "Big Sur . . ."), Freud also speaks of such a rapport in his *Interpretation of Dreams.*

7) It was in Freud's *Interpretation* that I read the account of his

own dream (which he analyzes) referred to in "Letter to a Young Father . . ." This poem also quotes Shakespeares' Sonnet Number 13 and cites a painting by Tintoretto entitled "The Origin of The Milky Way," which I am grateful to Dr. Zelda Teplitz for calling to my attention.

8) The quotation from Gabriel Marcel in ". . . on the Death of Cummings" is from his *Homo Viator.*

9) The quotation from the theologian F. W. Robertson as epigraph to "Lines for Michael . . ." was given me by Michael Rust from Robertson's journal. The photograph on which this poem is based was taken by Robert Sund, and was first published in England in "Agenda."

10) The reference to Bartleby in "Thirteen Preludes . . ." alludes to the fact that George Bluestone made a film based on Melville's story in an ancient building on Pioneer Square. This poem was first published in a college periodical at Eastern Washington University and then in "Literature in the Arts and Society."